The Beginner's Guide to Canadian Honours

The Beginner's Guide to Canadian Honours

Christopher McCreery

Foreword by His Royal Highness
The Prince Edward, Earl of Wessex

DUNDURN PRESS

TORONTO

Editor: Michael Carroll
Design: Jennifer Scott
Printer: Marquis

Library and Archives Canada Cataloguing in Publication

McCreery, Christopher
    The beginner's guide to Canadian honours / Christopher McCreery.

ISBN 978-1-55002-748-8

    1. Decorations of honour--Canada. 2. Awards--Canada. I. Title.

CR6257.M324 2008   929.8'171   C2008-900699-2

1   2   3   4   5   12   11   10   09   08

We acknowledge the support of the **Canada Council for the Arts** and the **Ontario Arts Council** for our publishing program. We also acknowledge the financial support of the **Government of Canada** through the **Book Publishing Industry Development Program** and **The Association for the Export of Canadian Books**, and the **Government of Ontario** through the **Ontario Book Publishers Tax Credit program**, and the **Ontario Media Development Corporation**.

Care has been taken to trace the ownership of copyright material used in this book. The author and the publisher welcome any information enabling them to rectify any references or credits in subsequent editions.

J. Kirk Howard, President

Printed and bound in Canada.
Printed on recycled paper.

www.dundurn.com

Dundurn Press
3 Church Street, Suite 500
Toronto, Ontario, Canada
M5E 1M2

Gazelle Book Services Limited
White Cross Mills
High Town, Lancaster, England
LA1 4XS

Dundurn Press
2250 Military Road
Tonawanda, NY
U.S.A. 14150

To my little brother, Jonathan

Her Majesty Queen Elizabeth II, Queen of Canada
Sovereign of the Order of Canada, Sovereign of the Order of Military Merit
Sovereign of the Order of Merit of the Police Forces.

Contents

His Royal Highness The Prince Edward, Earl of Wessex, KG, KCVO, SOM.

BAGSHOT PARK

We all know how important it is to say "thank you" to people who have helped us and served others. What is true for us as individuals is just as true for communities and nations. In this small but highly-informative book, Christopher McCreery explains how Canada thanks deserving citizens through honours of the Crown.

One of the roles of The Queen as Sovereign of Canada is to be the "fount of honours". Her Majesty authorises the creation of honours in Canada and sometimes personally confers them, although usually her representatives, the Governor General and the Lieutenant Governors, do this on her behalf. Dr. McCreery tells us what these honours are; he explains the distinction between orders, decorations and medals; he shows how recipients are nominated and selected; and he provides examples of Canadians who have been honoured for remarkable civic achievements, bravery and gallantry, voluntarism and meritorious service.

The Beginner's Guide to Canadian Honours also gives a brief history of how, after many years of using British awards, Canada created its own honours, starting with the Order of Canada in 1967 and developing into the comprehensive system Canadians enjoy today. Canada's distinctive honours of the Crown are now very much part of its national identity.

It is therefore with great personal pleasure that I commend Dr. McCreery's concise, well-illustrated book to all those, especially younger Canadians, who want to know more about Canada's rich, diverse and respected honours system. Regrettably it will not help you decipher most of the initials after my name, but it will reveal what SOM stands for, an honour of the Province of Saskatchewan that I was privileged to receive a few years ago.

Edward

His Royal Highness The Prince Edward, Earl of Wessex, KG, KCVO, SOM

Introduction

Almost every country in the world has an honours system. Although Canada is a relatively young country, we are fortunate to have one of the most complete honours systems in the world. Countries from Australia to Fiji have looked to Canada as a leader in this field. However, little has been written about our national honours system, how it operates, and who it recognizes.

I hope this book will be an easy read for people who wish to learn about the basics of the honours system and how it operates in Canada. It has been designed to meet the needs of people who know little or nothing about honours — orders, decorations, and medals. In Chapter 12, a "wearing guide" is also included.

Those wishing to gain a more detailed knowledge of Canada's various orders, decorations, and medals should consult my previous books, *The Canadian Honours System* or *The Order of Canada: Its Origins, History and Development*.

This book examines honours that are presented by the governor general on behalf of the Queen, meaning official awards from the government of Canada. Other unofficial awards — presented by schools, societies, and associations — are not examined here.

At the back of this book you will find a glossary containing some of the less-common words used in the text.

Her Excellency the Right Honourable Michaëlle Jean, CC, CMM, COM, CD, the governor general of Canada, wears the insignia of Prior of the Order of St. John.

Royal Arms of Canada

 # What Is an Honour?

Almost every country in the world has a means to recognize people who have done something outstanding to help others. The way a country says "thank you" is usually through an order, decoration, or medal — what are known as honours.

The monarch or leader of a country awards honours to those who have made significant contributions to helping others. Honours are also given to people who have acted bravely — trying to save someone caught in a house fire, for instance.

The ancient idea of honour is that people are truthful and loyal to their sovereign and are willing to defend the land in which they live. This is much like the idea of honour made famous through stories about King Arthur and the Knights of the Round Table.

Today honour still means to be truthful and loyal, but it also represents making a contribution to one's community or to people all over the world. For those serving in the Canadian Forces the idea of honour still includes a willingness to defend Canada. For this type of honour there are special awards such as the Victoria Cross, the Star of Military Valour, and the Order of Military Merit.

For civilians there are honours such as the Order of Canada and Meritorious Service Decorations. Citizens who make important contributions to their communities or to Canada as a whole can receive honours.

The three main types of honours are orders, decorations, and medals:

- **Orders:** These recognize outstanding achievement and exceptional service over a long period (in some cases a lifetime). The main orders in the Canadian honours system have different levels to recognize various types of service. People are "appointed" to be members of an order but are not "awarded" an order.

- **Decorations:** These recognize a specific act of bravery or meritorious service. There are three types of decorations:

  - **Military Valour:** Awarded for an act of courage in combat.
  - **Bravery:** Awarded for acts such as lifesaving.
  - **Meritorious Service Decorations:** Awarded for a specific act of meritorious service, not necessarily over a long period.

- **Medals:** These are the awards most often associated with honours. There are three types of medals:

  - **Campaign Service Medals:** These are awarded for service in a particular military mission or operation and are the medals we usually see veterans wearing on Remembrance Day.
  - **Commemorative Medals:** These are awarded on the occasion of a special event such as a coronation or a jubilee. Both civilians and members of the military can receive these.
  - **Long Service Medals:** These are awarded for long service and honourable conduct over a set period (twelve to twenty years).

Queen Elizabeth II presents the George Medal to Flight Lieutenant Robert Sabourin of the Royal Canadian Air Force at Rideau Hall in Ottawa on Dominion (Canada) Day in 1959.

In the Senate Chamber in the Centre Block on Parliament Hill in Ottawa in June 2006, the Honourable René Marin, chancellor of the Order of St. John, invests RCMP Constable Robert Rae Underhill as a Knight of Justice of the Order of St. John.

15

In Edmonton in May 2005, Queen Elizabeth II presents His Honour Norman Kwong, lieutenant-governor of Alberta, with the Order of St. John, while Her Honour Mary Kwong, the lieutenant-governor's wife, looks on.

2 Honours in Early Canada

CANADA'S NATIVE PEOPLES AND HONOURS

Canada's original people, the First Nations and Inuit, had their own types of awards and ways of recognizing people who made important contributions to their communities. One method to bestow an honour was to make a person a band chief. Native Canadians also had elaborate and beautiful bead belts and chest plates (a special shirt made of beads) that were presented to members of their bands who made significant contributions. Different bands and tribes also occasionally exchanged awards as a way of negotiating an agreement.

After the Europeans arrived, they copied the Native people by awarding Indian Chief Medals to the chiefs of tribes allied with them.

HONOURS IN NEW FRANCE

From 1534 to 1763, France controlled New France, which today makes up a large part of Canada. France, like most other nations in the world, awarded honours to those who helped to defend its territory.

In New France the King of France awarded the Order of St. Louis, known as the Croix St. Louis, for acts of loyalty and valiant military service. Like many modern awards, the Croix St. Louis was hung from a ribbon (so it could be worn on the chest or around the neck) and was made of precious metal (gold or silver).

More than two hundred French-Canadian soldiers received this award for helping to defend New France. Like most early honours, the Order of St. Louis was only awarded to soldiers, and no women received it.

BRITISH HONOURS IN CANADA

When the British defeated the French in North America and took over New France formally in 1763 after the Treaty of Paris, they brought their own system of honours. In 1867, with Confederation, most of Britain's Canadian colonies united into one dominion, Canada, within the British Empire. The new country's governor general wanted to start a Canadian honour called the Order of St. Lawrence. This new order was to be awarded for service specifically to Canada. However, the British government wouldn't allow this change and forced Canada to continue using the British honours system until 1967.

British honours awarded to Canadians had names such as the Order of the Bath and the Order of St. Michael and St. George. Many of the Fathers of Canadian Confederation were awarded British honours. The most famous was Prime Minister Sir John A. Macdonald, who was made a Knight Commander of the Order of the Bath. When he was knighted by Queen Victoria, he was allowed to put "Sir" in front of his name to indicate that he was a knight.

Other Canadians went on to receive British honours such as Sir Frederick Banting, the co-discoverer of insulin; Lucy Maud Montgomery, the author of *Anne of Green Gables*; and Dr. Wilder Penfield, the famous neurosurgeon. Nearly two million Canadians received different British awards (mostly war medals) between 1867 and 1967.

Flag of Royal France

The Croix St. Louis was awarded to residents of New France.

Flag of the United Kingdom

The Canada General Service Medal was awarded to soldiers who served in the Fenian raids of 1866 and 1870 and the Red River Rebellion of 1870.

Indian Chief Medal

Sir John A. Macdonald, Canada's first prime minister, was made a Knight Commander of the Order of the Bath in 1867.

Knight Commander of the Most Honourable Order of the Bath, Civil Division

Sir Frederick Banting, the co-discoverer of insulin, was made a Knight Commander of the Most Excellent Order of the British Empire in 1934.

The North West Canada Medal was awarded to soldiers who served in the North-West Rebellion of 1885.

3 Canada at War

It is important to look at Canada's involvement in the two world wars of the last century. It was during these wars that Canada began to develop its own identity and symbols, which eventually led to a desire to create a uniquely Canadian honours system.

FIRST WORLD WAR, 1914–1918

During the First World War, more than six hundred thousand Canadian men and women served all over the world. Canada used British honours to recognize the bravery, gallantry, and meritorious service that many of these individuals displayed.

For soldiers who performed gallant acts there was the Victoria Cross (VC). Perhaps the most famous Canadian to be awarded the VC was the air ace Billy Bishop. There were also more junior bravery awards such as the navy's Distinguished Service Cross, the army's Military Cross, and the air force's Distinguished Flying Cross.

Women were also recognized for the first time. Although they weren't allowed to fight in combat, many served as nurses. A number of Canadian nurses were awarded the Royal Red

Cross for their distinguished service and, in some cases, bravery.

Soldiers who fought in the First World War were also awarded military service medals. Most of them received the 1914–1918 British War Medal and the Victory Medal.

SECOND WORLD WAR, 1939–1945

When the Second World War started in 1939, the Canadian government decided that Canada would continue to use British honours to recognize bravery, gallantry, and distinguished service. These were the same awards used during the First World War.

A Canadian honour was finally created in 1943, midway through the war. After a long debate, Prime Minister William Lyon Mackenzie King and King George VI agreed to initiate the Canada Medal. It was to be awarded to Canadians who rendered important service during the war. Although the medal was established, it was never awarded because the government couldn't decide who should receive it.

As in the First World War, medals were awarded to those who served overseas. Canadians received the Defence Medal, the Canadian Volunteer Service Medal, the 1939–45 Star, the Burma Star, the France and Germany Star, and a number of others. More than one million Canadian men and women served at home and overseas during the Second World War.

During the Second World War, more than two thousand Canadians, both military and civilian, who had performed important work, were appointed to the Order of the British Empire. In many ways this order served as the Order of Canada before 1967.

KOREAN WAR, 1950–1953

More than fifteen thousand Canadian men and women served in the Korean War, helping the United Nations defend South Korea. During this period, Canadians continued to receive British awards for bravery and gallantry.

Canadians who served in the Korean War received the Korea War Medal, the Canadian Volunteer Medal for Korea, and the United Nations Service Medal for Korea.

Canada's flag during the First World War.

A trio of First World War medals: the 1914–15 Star, the British War Medal, and the Allied Victory Medal.

Distinguished Conduct Medal

Military Medal

Distinguished Flying Cross

Canada's flag during the Second World War.

Above Left: *Reverse of the Canada Medal*

Above Right: *Obverse of the Canada Medal*

A group of Second World War medals: 1939–45 Star, France and Germany Star, Defence Medal, Canadian Volunteer Service Medal, 1939–45 War Medal, Efficiency Medal (for long service), and French Croix de Guerre (for gallantry).

Order of the British Empire   *The Royal Canadian Navy sees action during the Second World War.*

Canadian Army tanks roll down a road in the Second World War.

In June 1940 in France, Royal Air Force pilots of 87 Squadron scramble to reach their Hurricanes.

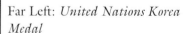

Above: *Korea Voluntary Service Medal*

Far Left: *United Nations Korea Medal*

Left: *A Canadian Second World War veteran displays his many medals.*

4 The Order of Canada: Centre of the Honours System

Following the end of the Korean War, there was some discussion about whether or not Canada should establish its own honours system. No agreement was reached, and it was decided that Canada would have no honours system at all, aside from a few long service medals. Awards of British honours effectively came to an end at this time.

This policy changed in 1966 when Prime Minister Lester B. Pearson determined that it was time for Canada to inaugurate its own honours system. Pearson was keenly interested in seeing Canada adopt new symbols of nationhood. He played, for example, a central role in the adoption of the Maple Leaf flag in 1965.

Prime Minister Pearson wasn't alone in thinking it was time to begin rewarding people who had helped to build modern Canada. Other influential Canadians such as Vincent Massey, the former governor general, worked hard to ensure the creation of a Canadian honour. After a great deal of debate, the government sanctioned the establishment of a new honour called the Order of Canada.

The Queen agreed with the prime minister and was pleased that Canada was finally going to set up its own honours system. Since the Queen is Canada's head of state, she was asked if she would become the sovereign or head of the Order of Canada. The governor general, who represents the Queen in Canada, was asked to become the chancellor of the order. Once the

Queen agreed to create the Order of Canada, other details had to be dealt with. Chief among these was what the insignia of the order was to look like.

The designer put a great deal of thought into the project but was unable to decide what shape to make the insignia (or badge). He knew it should have a maple leaf (similar to the one on Canada's flag) and a crown (representing the Queen and Canada's sovereignty). Finally, while walking home on a snowy November day, the designer came up with an idea: "Why not make the badge the same shape as a snowflake?"

The symbolism was perfect. Canada is known for being a snowy place in winter, and each snowflake is different, just like the various individuals who would be appointed to the Order of Canada.

The next challenge was to choose a ribbon for the order. Every order is worn from a different ribbon, whether it is displayed around the neck or on the breast. The prime minister decided that the ribbon should be the same as the new Canadian flag — red-white-red.

Within a short time the design was complete and Canada finally had its own honour — the Order of Canada. The next important question to be dealt with was who should receive the new honour.

HOW ARE PEOPLE APPOINTED TO THE ORDER OF CANADA?

When the Order of Canada was launched in 1967, it was decided that it should be given to Canadians who made important contributions to "Canada and humanity at large." This is the main reason the motto of the order is *Desiderantes meliorem patriam*, which is Latin for "They desire a better country."

To make the selection process fair and to avoid political interference, a special body of people was established. With the co-operation of the Chancellery of Honours at Rideau Hall (the governor general's residence in Ottawa), this group, called the Advisory Council, recommends candidates for appointment to the order. The council makes its recommendations to the Queen through the governor general and consists of people such as the chief justice of the Supreme Court, the chair of the Canada Council for the Arts, the clerk of the Privy Council, the deputy minister of heritage, and a number of members of the Order of Canada. Staff officials at the Chancellery ask people from all over Canada to nominate fellow citizens for the order and then use that information as the basis of recommendations.

Every year nearly a thousand Canadians write to the Chancellery to nominate members of their communities to receive the Order of Canada. These nominations are reviewed by the Chancellery and then additional research into the work of the nominees is done.

The Advisory Council meets twice a year to review the nominations and decide who should be recommended to receive the Order of Canada. After the Advisory Council makes its decisions, it submits the Order of Canada Recommendation List to the governor general. The governor general then approves this list on behalf of the Queen. The list is published twice a year.

Once the list is approved, confidential letters are sent to the proposed recipients. The letters inform them that they have been chosen to receive the order and inquire if they are willing to accept. The letters also ask the recipients not to tell anyone until their appointments are announced by the governor general.

Twice a year the governor general reveals the names of people who have been appointed to the Order of Canada. Recipients are invited to attend a ceremony at Rideau Hall to receive their insignia from the governor general at a special investiture ceremony. When people are given their insignia of the Order of Canada at the investiture ceremony, citations are read out. These citations explain why the recipients have been appointed to the Order of Canada.

In addition to the insignia of the Order of Canada, recipients receive a certificate and a lapel badge. The lapel badge is intended to be worn every day, while there are only a few occasions a year when it is appropriate to wear the full-size insignia of the Order of Canada.

WHO ADMINISTERS THE ORDER OF CANADA?

The Order of Canada is administered by a variety of officials. Each one has a specific job that helps to ensure that worthy Canadians are appointed to the order. Most of the work is done by the Chancellery of Honours, which is part of the governor general's office at Rideau Hall. Those who take part include:

- The **sovereign** is the Queen of Canada, Queen Elizabeth II. She is the head of the Order of Canada and the entire Canadian honours system.
- The **chancellor** is the governor general of Canada. The chancellor is in charge of approving the Order of Canada Honours List and bestowing the Order of Canada insignia at investitures.
- The **secretary general** is in charge of all work to arrange the investiture ceremonies and the meetings of the Advisory Council.
- The **Advisory Council** is the group of Canadians who recommend to the Queen and the governor general who should receive the Order of Canada. They read through the nomination letters and decide who is most deserving of the order.
- The **Chancellery staff** consists of the officials who read through the nomination forms when they are first received. Chancellery staff members put together additional information and biographies of each nominee for the Advisory Council to read.
- The **nominators** are Canadian citizens who write to the Advisory Council to inform it about people they feel are worthy of appointment to the Order of Canada.

WHO HAS BEEN APPOINTED TO THE ORDER OF CANADA?

More than five thousand people from across Canada have been appointed to the Order of Canada since 1967. Recipients include:

- Wayne Gretzky, the famous hockey player.
- Raffi Cavoukian, the children's singer.
- Marc Garneau and Roberta Bondar, astronauts.
- Terry Fox, a brave young man with cancer who was overtaken by the disease halfway

through an attempt to run across Canada on one good leg and a prosthesis to raise money for cancer research.

- Michel Cailloux, the children's storyteller.
- Rick Hansen, the man who wheeled his wheelchair around the world to raise money for spinal cord research.
- Robertson Davies, the author of the novel *Fifth Business* and numerous other books.
- Lester B. Pearson, the former Canadian prime minister who also won the Nobel Peace Prize in 1957.
- Anne Ottenbrite, the first Canadian female swimmer to win a gold medal at the Summer Olympics (in 1984), and the youngest person still, at eighteen, ever appointed to the Order of Canada.

Listed below are a few examples of people in a variety of fields who have been appointed to the Order of Canada:

- Elizabeth May, a well-known environmentalist, was made an Officer of the Order of Canada in 2005. She was cited as "a respected voice for Canada's environmental movement for more than 30 years. Sought out nationally and beyond our borders, she has been involved with organizations concerned with natural resource management, sustainable development and the protection of global ecosystems. She has also contributed to the creation of several national parks, the implementation of pollution control measures and to the drafting of environmental legislation."
- Jean Vanier was first appointed an Officer of the Order of Canada and was later elevated to Companion of the Order of Canada. When someone moves from one level of the order to another, it is known as a promotion. Part of Vanier's citation reads: "This theologian and philosopher has chosen to devote his life to promoting the well-being, development and social integration of physically and mentally disabled adults by founding the Fédération internationale de l'Arche which encompasses a large number of homes and workshops throughout the world."

- Roméo Dallaire, the former Canadian Forces general and now a member of the Canadian Senate, was made an Officer of the Order of Canada in 2002. His citation, in part, reads: "He served with great distinction in the Canadian Forces for over 30 years and continues to be a model of dedication and selflessness. Throughout his illustrious career, he held a variety of appointments in Canada and abroad, including commander of the United Nations Missions to Uganda and Rwanda where he displayed exceptional professionalism and superb leadership. Now retired, he has accepted new challenges as special advisor to the Canadian International Development Agency on matters relating to war-affected children."

- Arthur MacKinnon was made a Member of the Order of Canada in 1989 for his volunteer and community service in Prince Edward Island. His citation describes him as a "retired school teacher devoted to his Prince Edward Island community [who] has generously spent countless hours caring for the visually impaired, the learning disabled, multiple sclerosis patients and senior citizens. He is an outstanding volunteer, always willing to organize a variety of outings, visit with hospital patients or nursing home residents, and to help with employment programs for the disabled."

- Dr. Jean Couture was made a Member of the Order of Canada in 1994. His citation said he was a "professor of surgery at Université Laval [who] has made a great contribution to specialized training in medicine and surgery and [who] has also helped establish quality standards for Canadian hospitals. Among other activities, he heads an international co-operation project that established an oncology unit at Norman Bethune University in China."

As can be seen from a couple of the names above, the order is for more than just famous Canadians. Most people who have received the order work at the local level.

Even non-Canadians have been given the Order of Canada in recognition of the things they have done for Canada and the whole world. One example is Nelson Mandela, the former president of South Africa who helped end apartheid and brought freedom to his country. Mandela was appointed an honorary Companion of the Order of Canada. In his citation he is called "a universal symbol of triumph over oppression who has inspired people everywhere to work peacefully to end intolerance and injustice. A towering figure in the transition from apartheid to democracy in South Africa, he has emerged as one of this century's greatest statesmen and humanitarians, recognized the world over for his dignity, moral strength, and integrity. His lifelong struggle for freedom, justice, and equality guarantees his presence in the history books of generations to come."

LEVELS OF THE ORDER OF CANADA

Depending on whether the contribution being recognized is local, national, or international in scope, an individual can be appointed to a different level of the Order of Canada. There are three levels: Companion (CC), Officer (OC), and Member (CM).

Companion

This is the highest level of the Order of Canada. A maximum of 165 living Canadians can be Companions of the Order of Canada. People are appointed Companions for outstanding achievement and merit of the greatest degree, especially service to Canada or to humanity at large. Companions of the Order of Canada receive an insignia made of gold and enamel that they wear around their necks. It has a red maple leaf in the centre.

Officer

This is the second-highest level of the Order of Canada. A maximum of sixty-four Canadians can be made Officers of the Order of Canada in a year. People are appointed Officers for achievement and merit of a high degree, especially service to Canada or to humanity at large.

Like Companions, Officers receive an insignia made of gold and enamel that they wear around their necks. The insignia is slightly smaller than the badge given to Companions, and the maple leaf in the centre is gold.

Member

This level of the Order of Canada is given to a maximum of 136 Canadians a year. People are appointed Members of the Order of Canada for distinguished service in or to a particular locality, group, or field of activity. People who are made Members of the Order of Canada receive an insignia fashioned from silver and enamel that they wear on their left breasts. The maple leaf in the centre of the badge is silver.

WHY ARE THERE THREE LEVELS?

The Order of Canada has different levels because of the many types of contributions Canadians make. Some Canadians undertake work that helps millions of people. Others make contributions on a smaller scale that help fellow citizens in their communities or professions. One of the principles of the Canadian honours system is that it is important to recognize all types of contributions, whether they are at the local, national, or international levels.

The Maple Leaf flag of Canada was officially adopted on February 15, 1965.

Queen Elizabeth II walks with Governor General Roland Michener shortly after the establishment of the Order of Canada in 1967.

A postcard from Expo 67 shows the inverted pyramid of the Canada Pavilion.

Companion of the Order of
Canada

Member of the Order of Canada

Officer of the Order of Canada

The Chancellor and Principal Companion
of the Order of Canada

Le Chancelier et Compagnon principal
de l'Ordre du Canada

To à   Joyce Turpin, B.E.M.

Greeting:

Salut:

Whereas, with the approval of Her Majesty Queen Elizabeth the Second, Sovereign of the Order of Canada, We have been pleased to appoint you to be a Member of the Order of Canada

We do by these Presents appoint you to be a Member of the said Order and authorize you to hold and enjoy the dignity of such appointment together with membership in the said Order and all privileges thereunto appertaining

Given at Rideau Hall in the City of Ottawa under the Seal of the Order of Canada this seventeenth day of December 1973.

By the Chancellor's Command.

Attendu que, avec l'assentiment de Sa Majesté la Reine Elizabeth Deux, Souveraine de l'Ordre du Canada, il Nous a plu de vous nommer Membre de l'Ordre du Canada

Nous vous nommons par les présentes Membre dudit Ordre et Nous vous autorisons à bénéficier et à jouir de la dignité de telle nomination ainsi que du titre de membre dudit Ordre et de tous les privilèges y afférents

Fait à Rideau Hall, dans la ville d'Ottawa, sous le Sceau de l'Ordre du Canada, ce dix-septième jour de décembre 1973.

Par ordre du Chancelier.

Le Secrétaire général de l'Ordre du Canada

Secretary General of the Order of Canada

Order of Canada certificate

Motto of the Order Canada

This Order of Canada insignia is worn by Queen Elizabeth II, who is the sovereign of the order.

A group of Canadian medals (left to right): Member of the Order of Canada, British Empire Medal, Defence Medal, Canadian Volunteer Service Medal, 1939–1945 War Medal, 1953 Queen Elizabeth II Coronation Medal, 1977 Queen Elizabeth II Silver Jubilee Medal, 1992 Canada 125th Anniversary of Confederation Medal, and 2002 Queen Elizabeth II Golden Jubilee Medal.

Canada's governor general, who is the chancellor of the Order of Canada, wears this insignia.

Companion of the Order of Canada Lapel Badge

Officer of the Order of Canada Lapel Badge

Member of the Order of Canada Lapel Badge

41

Marathoner Terry Fox displays the Companion of the Order of Canada that he received on September 18, 1980.

Wheelchair athlete Rick Hansen is invested as an Officer of the Order of Canada on June 29, 1987.

Noted South African Nelson Mandela (left) was appointed an honorary Companion of the Order of Canada in September 1998.

Novelist Margaret Atwood (left) is invested as a Companion of the Order of Canada on November 6, 1988.

Hockey superstar Wayne Gretzky is invested as an Officer of the Order of Canada on January 28, 1998.

5 Other Canadian Orders

The Order of Canada isn't the only order in the Canadian honours system. Indeed, there are four other orders. These orders recognize specific service to an organization or group. As with the Order of Canada, people are "appointed" to the other Canadian orders.

ORDER OF MILITARY MERIT

Presented to members of the Canadian Forces who have performed important services in the navy, army, and air force, the Order of Military Merit can be thought of as an Order of Canada for Canada's military. This order was founded in 1972, and about one hundred Canadians receive it every year.

Like the Order of Canada, the Order of Military Merit has three levels: Commander (CMM), Officer (OMM), and Member (MMM). The degree of responsibility a person has determines the level to which he or she may be appointed.

Only a small number (less than one-tenth of one percent) of members of the Canadian Forces are appointed to the Order of Military Merit. Recipients are chosen by a special advisory committee.

ORDER OF MERIT OF THE POLICE FORCES

The Order of Merit of the Police Forces is similar to the Order of Military Merit. It differs in that only police officers can be recipients. This order is the newest one in the Canadian honours system. It was founded by the Queen in 2000. Approximately fifty police officers are appointed each year. The order has three levels: Commander (COM), Officer (OOM), and Member (MOM).

ROYAL VICTORIAN ORDER

Created by Queen Victoria in 1896, the Royal Victorian Order is one of the oldest elements of the Canadian honours system. Those Canadians who assist the Queen, members of the royal family, the governor general, or lieutenant-governors are sometimes awarded the Royal Victorian Order in recognition of their important service to the Canadian Crown.

The order has three levels in Canada; Commander (CVO), lieutenant (LVO) and member (MVO). Appointments to the Royal Victorian Order are usually made during royal visits, and it is the most sparingly bestowed Canadian order.

ORDER OF ST. JOHN

The Order of St. John has been active in Canada since 1883. It is a volunteer organization that operates worldwide. In Canada the order runs the St. John Ambulance, teaches first aid, and undertakes a variety of charitable works. The order also operates an eye hospital in Jerusalem. The Canadian part of the order also raises money to help fund the hospital and a variety of health programs throughout Africa. Canadians are appointed to this order for exceptional service to the charitable works of the Order of St. John.

PROVINCIAL ORDERS

Each Canadian province has an order that, like the Order of Canada, recognizes lifetime achievement. These orders are an important way for individual provinces to reward citizens for outstanding service at the local and provincial level. The names of the provincial orders are as follows:

- L'Ordre national du Québec
- Saskatchewan Order of Merit
- Order of Ontario
- Order of British Columbia
- Alberta Order of Excellence
- Order of Manitoba
- Order of Prince Edward Island
- Order of New Brunswick
- Order of Nova Scotia
- Order of Newfoundland and Labrador

In most provinces the lieutenant-governor presents the order, and recipients receive an insignia, award certificate, and lapel badge. Canadians appointed to the provincial orders are chosen by special advisory councils or committees just as recipients of the Order of Canada are.

Top Left: *Commander of the Order of Military Merit*

Top Centre: *Officer of the Order of Military Merit*

Top Right: *Member of the Order of Military Merit*

Bottom Left: *Commander of the Order of Merit of the Police Forces*

Bottom Right: *Officer of the Order of Merit of the Police Forces*

Member of the Order of Merit of the Police Forces

Lieutenant of the Royal Victorian Order

Commander of the Royal Victorian Order

Member of the Royal Victorian Order

Royal Victorian Medal

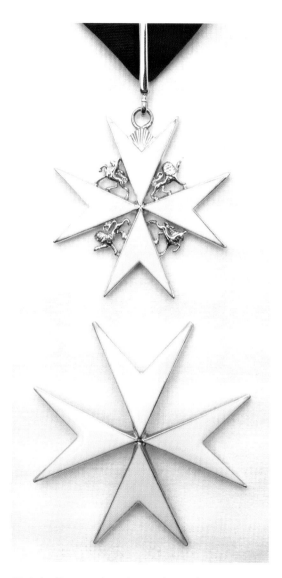

Serving Member of the
Order of St. John

Knight/Dame of Justice of the Order of St. John

Chevalier of L'Ordre national du Québec

Saskatchewan Order of Merit

Order of Ontario

Order of British Columbia

Alberta Order of Excellence

Order of Prince Edward Island

Order of New Brunswick

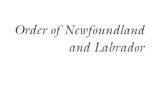

Order of Manitoba

Order of Nova Scotia

*Order of Newfoundland
and Labrador*

6 Military Valour and Bravery Decorations

The Order of Canada is part of the wider Canadian honour system that comprises many different awards. Included in our honours system are military valour and bravery awards, which are bestowed on individuals who perform extraordinary acts of self-sacrifice and bravery.

Canada has six different gallantry and bravery awards. They are given to people who demonstrate great courage and high regard for others in civilian life or while serving with the Canadian Forces (navy, army, and air force) in an armed conflict.

VICTORIA CROSS (VC)

This award is the oldest in the Canadian honours system. It was created by Queen Victoria in 1856 to be granted to members of the Commonwealth armed forces "for most conspicuous bravery or some daring or pre-eminent act of valour or self-sacrifice or extreme devotion to duty in the presence of the enemy." A total of ninety-four Canadians have been awarded the Victoria Cross. Most were conferred during the two world wars.

A First World War air ace ranks among the most famous Canadians to receive the medal. Billy Bishop was awarded the VC "for most conspicuous bravery, determination and skill. Captain

Bishop, who had been sent out to work independently, flew first of all to an enemy aerodrome; finding no machine about, he flew on to another aerodrome about three miles south-east, which was at least twelve miles the other side of the line." Bishop found seven enemy aircraft on the ground and managed to destroy a number of them in the air and on the field.

VICTORIA CROSS (CANADA)

In 1993 the Queen established the Victoria Cross (Canada) to recognize "most conspicuous bravery or some daring or pre-eminent act of valour or self-sacrifice in the presence of the enemy." No VC (Canada) has yet been awarded. It is important to note that "enemy" is interpreted to mean "a hostile force, including armed mutineers, armed rebels, armed rioters and armed pirates." Thus Canada doesn't have to be in a formal state of war (just an armed conflict) for members of the Canadian Forces to be eligible for the Victoria Cross. The VC (Canada) is made in part from the same metal that the original Victoria Cross was made of and includes copper from an 1867 Confederation Medal along with metallic elements taken from every Canadian province and territory.

STAR OF MILITARY VALOUR AND MEDAL OF MILITARY VALOUR

Like the Victoria Cross, the Star of Military Valour (SMV) and the Medal of Military Valour (MMV) are given to members of the Canadian Forces who perform a brave act (defending their unit) in a warlike situation. It was only in 2006 that these medals began to be awarded. They have been presented to members of the Canadian Forces for their part in stabilizing Afghanistan.

Major William Fletcher was awarded the Star of Military Valour in February 2007. He "repeatedly demonstrated extraordinary bravery by exposing himself to intense fire while leading his forces, on foot, to assault heavily defended enemy positions. On two occasions, the soldiers at his side were struck by enemy fire. He immediately rendered first aid and then continued to head the subsequent assaults. On these occasions and in ensuing combat actions, his selfless courage, tactical acumen and effective command were pivotal to the success of his company in defeating a determined opponent."

Corporal John Makela was awarded the Medal of Military Valour in February 2007. "On 16 October 2006, Corporal Makela prevented a fatal attack on his combat logistics patrol by a suicide bomber in Afghanistan. As the turret gunner providing overwatch for the convoy, he accurately identified the approaching suspicious vehicle as a suicide bomber car. Despite the likely potential of an explosion, he maintained his exposed position and applied fire, resulting in the premature detonation of the bomber car. The explosion engulfed Corporal Makela's vehicle and seriously burned him. His valiant and courageous actions inevitably prevented the bomber from reaching his intended target and saved the lives of the other soldiers in the convoy."

CROSS OF VALOUR

The Cross of Valour (CV) was created in 1972 and is awarded to Canadian civilians and members of the Canadian Forces for "acts of the most conspicuous courage in circumstances of extreme peril." It is Canada's highest honour for civilian bravery. In all, twenty Canadians have been presented with the Cross of Valour.

Anna Ruth Lang of New Brunswick was awarded the CV in 1982. "In the early afternoon of 9 September 1980, Anna Lang displayed selfless courage to a very high degree in the rescue of her two car passengers. At the entry of the Hammond River Bridge a fuel tanker hit Mrs. Lang's car and rammed it through the railing into the river. The tanker then fell into the river and exploded. Despite a concussion, rapidly-spreading fire, and the threat of further explosion, Mrs. Lang swam to shore, removed her heavy clothing, and returned to the submerged car. At great risk to her life, she reached her passengers through a wall of fire on the surface of the water. With much difficulty she dragged a woman and her four-year-old son a safe distance from the roaring inferno, and continued with both toward shore until two young men came to assist. She suffered extensive burns during the rescue."

STAR OF COURAGE AND MEDAL OF BRAVERY

The Star of Courage (SC) and the Medal of Bravery (MB) are awarded to people who perform a brave act in the face of great danger. People who run into burning buildings or jump into fast-running water to save others often receive these honours.

New Brunswicker Sharon O'Brien was presented with the Star of Courage in 1981. "On 6 December 1979, Mrs. Sharon O'Brien saved her four-year-old son from drowning in the Saint John River. With his friend, Mrs. O'Brien's son was playing in a rowboat when it was cast adrift by a high wind. Some hundred and fifty feet from shore the boys panicked and leapt into the icy water. Alerted to the danger by an elder son, Mrs. O'Brien telephoned for help, ran to the river's edge and swam out to the children. She was not, however, able to reach her son's friend before he drowned but brought her boy in. He was taken to hospital and recovered from his ordeal."

Herman Ho was awarded the Medal of Bravery in 1995. "Mr. Ho rescued a man from drowning in the Fraser River on 22 November 1993, in Vancouver, British Columbia. While jogging, Mr. Ho heard calls for help and saw a man being carried downstream by the current. He quickly entered the cold, murky water and, although not a strong swimmer, managed to reach the victim. The man began struggling with his rescuer, but Mr. Ho was able to calm him and towed him some seventy-five metres back to shore, where he administered first aid."

Russell Reid, William Nicol, and George Porter were given the Medal of Bravery in 1993 for disarming a bank robber. "Noticing him at the next wicket, Mr. Reid grabbed the man's wrist and tried to wrench the firearm from his grasp. Unfortunately, the thief managed to turn the gun on Mr. Reid and shot him. Mr. Nicol grabbed the revolver and the robber's hand, forcing it down, while Mr. Porter charged at the bandit. Together, they managed to wrestle the bank robber to the floor and, with the aid of other customers, disarmed him and held him until the police arrived."

The British Victoria Cross has been awarded to ninety-four Canadians from the Crimean War to the Second World War.

Star of Military Valour

The Canadian Victoria Cross was established in 1993. None have been awarded thus far.

Medal of Military Valour

Cross of Valour

Medal of Bravery

Star of Courage

7 Meritorious Service Decorations

People who perform a specific exemplary act are awarded meritorious service decorations. There are two decorations: the Meritorious Service Cross (MSC) and the Meritorious Service Medal (MSM).

These medals are awarded for contributions of a specific nature. The MSC and MSM differ from the Order of Canada in that the Order of Canada is usually awarded for a lifetime of achievement. Both members of the military and civilians can receive meritorious service decorations. A few examples of meritorious service decoration recipients follow.

Silken Laumann was awarded the Meritorious Service Cross in 1993. "At the 1992 Olympic Games, Ms. Laumann triumphed over an extremely serious leg injury to win the Bronze Medal in the women's single rowing competition. Thanks to her tremendous courage and determination, she was able to defy the odds and continue a brilliant athletic career that had already been marked in 1991 by the world championship title and a first place in the World Cup."

Sergeant Thomas Hoppe received the Meritorious Service Cross in 1994 while serving in Bosnia during a United Nations peacekeeping mission. "Sergeant Hoppe was the commander of a key observation post located between Serb and Muslim forces in Bosnia-Herzegovina.

On several occasions, the post came under direct, aimed, small-arms and anti-armour fire in July 1994. Conscious of the need to maintain his position of observation of the opposing forces, he moved his armoured vehicles while preparing to return fire to safeguard his men and carry out his task."

George Spittael was awarded the Meritorious Service Medal in 1993. "Since the Second World War, Mr. Spittael, a Belgian citizen, has provided exceptional humanitarian service for Canadian families, by researching and documenting the grave sites of military personnel buried overseas during both World Wars. His efforts have brought peace of mind to many families. Now in his sixties, Mr. Spittael continues to guide Canadians to various cemeteries and battlefields of Europe."

In 1997 Nancy Malloy was given the Meritorious Service Medal posthumously for her humanitarian work. "From September 1996 until her brutal murder in December 1996, Ms. Malloy was the Medical Administrator of the Red Cross Hospital in Novye Atagi, Chechnya. An outstanding humanitarian, Ms. Malloy volunteered for overseas assignments with the International Committee of the Red Cross (ICRC). An optimistic and compassionate individual, Ms. Malloy selflessly devoted her life to providing assistance to conflict victims of war-torn countries."

Daniel Bellemare received the Meritorious Service Medal in 2003 for his work in government. "In his capacity as Assistant Deputy Attorney General, Daniel Bellemare has played a leading role, on behalf of Canada, in the creation in 1995 of the International Association of Prosecutors. Thanks to his efforts, his dedication and his involvement in the Association's activities, Mr. Bellemare has contributed to increasing the understanding of the prosecutors' role while promoting international cooperation on criminal justice and human rights issues."

Meritorious Service Cross
(Military Division)

Meritorious Service Medal
(Civil Division)

8 Military Campaign and Service Medals

There are dozens of different types of military service medals. This section provides an overview of the main ones. A chart containing all the different Canadian order, decoration, and medal ribbons can be found in Chapter 13.

For hundreds of years members of the navy and army who fought in specific battles or wars have received medals in recognition of their service. The first modern medal (a silver disc hung from a ribbon) was awarded following the Battle of Waterloo in 1815. Since that time, all Canadian medals and most medals around the world have followed this general design.

As discussed in Chapter 3, Canadians have been receiving military service medals, which are often called war medals, since the War of 1812. Today there are many different types of military service medals, a reflection of Canada's involvement in many nations around the world and its participation in international organizations such as the United Nations and the North Atlantic Treaty Organization (NATO) in peacekeeping, peacemaking, and other assistance missions.

For members of the Canadian Forces who serve in the High Arctic there is the Special Service Medal with a bar bearing the word *ALERT*. Those who served in Germany from the 1950s to the 1990s received the Special Service Medal with the bar bearing the NATO star, flanked by the word *NATO* and its French equivalent, *OTAN*. Peacekeepers are often awarded different United Nations peacekeeping service medals. They also receive the Canadian Peacekeeping Service Medal.

Canadians who served in the First Gulf War (1990–91) were awarded the Gulf and Kuwait War Medal. Many Canadians served in the former Yugoslavia in the 1990s to help bring stability to the region. Because this mission was directed by NATO, Canadians received a NATO service medal. Canadians who have served in Afghanistan and in the war on terror receive the South-West Asia Service Medal, the General Campaign Star, or the General Service Medal.

Military service medals generally follow a standard design. The image shown on the obverse (front) of the medal is "who the medal is from" — the Queen and Canada, for example. The reverse (back) of the medal shows "what the medal is for."

Waterloo Medal *Gulf and Kuwait Medal* *Somalia Medal*

General Service Medal

*Peacekeeping Service
Medal*

General Campaign Star

United Nations Emergency Force Medal

*United Nations
Truce Supervision
Organization in
Palestine Medal*

United Nations
Peacekeeping Force in
Cyprus Medal

NATO Kosovo Medal

United Nations
Disengagement
Observation Force
(Golan Heights) Medal

Special Service Medal

Multinational Force and
Observers Medal

9 Commemorative Medals

The idea behind commemorative medals can be traced back more than five hundred years to the Indian state of Pudukkottai where the ruler presented *khelates* — small medals — to loyal subjects on special occasions. Commemorative medals are created to celebrate a special anniversary. They are awarded only during the year of celebration. For example, during the one hundredth and twenty-fifth anniversary of Confederation a medal was presented to forty-two thousand Canadians. Most recently, in 2002, to celebrate the fiftieth anniversary of Queen Elizabeth II as Canada's head of state, a golden jubilee medal was given to forty-six thousand Canadians. These types of commemorative medals have been awarded to Canadians since Queen Victoria's Golden Jubilee in 1887.

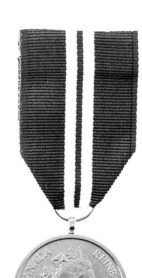

King George V Coronation Medal (1911)

Queen Victoria Diamond Jubilee Medal (1897)

Queen Elizabeth II Golden Jubilee Medal (2002)

Queen Elizabeth II Coronation Medal (1953)

Members of the Canadian Militia parade during the coronation of King George V in 1911.

*Canada Centennial
Medal (1967)*

*Queen Elizabeth II
Silver Jubilee (1977)
Medal*

*125th Anniversary of
Confederation (1992)
Medal*

10 Long Service Medals

For Canadians who put their lives on the line every day to protect fellow citizens, there are a number of long service medals. These are awarded to members of the Canadian Forces (navy, army, and air force) and the Royal Canadian Mounted Police (RCMP), as well as to peace officers (Canada Border Services Agency or Parks Canada staff, for instance), paramedics, correctional officers, firefighters, people serving in the Coast Guard, and members of other police forces.

Members of the Canadian Forces receive the Canadian Force's Decoration after twelve years of service and good conduct. RCMP members are given the Royal Canadian Mounted Police Long Service Medal after twenty years of service. Members of other police forces, correctional services, fire departments, the Coast Guard, paramedic services, and peace organizations are awarded a variety of exemplary service medals for twenty years of long and exemplary service.

Efficiency Decoration

Territorial Decoration

Royal Canadian Mounted Police Long Service and Good Conduct Medal

Army Long Service and Good Conduct Medal

Canadian Forces Decoration

Police Exemplary
Service Medal

Corrections Exemplary
Service Medal

Fire Services
Exemplary Service
Medal

Canadian Coast
Guard Exemplary
Service Medal

Emergency Medical
Services Exemplary
Service Medal

Peace Officer Exemplary Service Medal

11 Other Awards

Aside from the orders, decorations, and medals outlined in previous chapters, other honours are awarded to Canadians. For example, the Queen's Medal for Champion Shot is presented to the most proficient marksman in the Canadian Forces and the RCMP.

Some provinces also award special medals. In Ontario there is the Ontario Good Citizenship Medal, while Saskatchewan has the Saskatchewan Volunteer Medal. Both of these awards are presented to people who have made significant contributions to volunteerism in their community. In 2005 Alberta and Saskatchewan struck special centennial medals to commemorate the hundredth anniversary of their entrance into Confederation and gave them to citizens who made significant contributions.

Although the Canadian Memorial Cross isn't an honour, it is a memento presented to the spouse (wife or husband) and parents of a member of the Canadian Forces who has been killed in the line of duty. The first Memorial Crosses were awarded at the end of the First World War to mothers and wives of Canadians killed in that conflict.

Commonwealth and foreign awards are given to Canadians who have performed some distinguished act that helped the country bestowing the honour. Canadians have received medals from the United States, Britain, France, Germany, Australia, Poland, Jamaica, China, and many other nations.

Queen's Medal for Champion Shot

Order of St. John Service Medal

Saskatchewan Centennial (2005) Medal

Saskatchewan Volunteer Medal

Alberta Centennial (2005) Medal

The Canadian Memorial Cross, King George V version, was issued during the First World War.

France's Chevalier de la Légion d'honneur

Officer of the Order of the Legion of Merit (United States)

12 When to Wear Your Medals

There are specific occasions when people who have orders, decorations, and medals are supposed to wear their awards. This chapter outlines the details of when to wear medals.

FULL-SIZE AND MINIATURE MEDALS

Full-size medals are those officially presented to a person by the government. These are worn during the daytime, while miniature medals are typically worn during the evening with formal dress. Miniature medals are small replicas of the full-size decoration and must be purchased privately. They are not usually provided by the government.

Dinner Jacket

Men (Black Tie)

The miniature insignia of all orders, decorations, and medals should be worn suspended from a medal bar attached to the left lapel of the coat. Only one full-size neck badge should be worn, suspended from a miniature-width ribbon. The ribbon is worn under the band of the tie so that the badge hangs three centimetres below the bow. A miniature of this badge should be included in those worn on the medal bar. Only one star of an order should be worn on the left side of the coat.

Women (Long Evening Dress)

The miniature insignia of all orders, decorations, and medals should be worn suspended from a medal bar attached to the left side of the dress. If in possession of only one such award, it may be worn on a bow. Only one full-size neck badge should be worn. This should be worn at the neck or on a bow above the medal bar on the left shoulder. Only one star of an order should be worn on the left side of the dress.

Morning Dress

Men (Tailcoat or Director's Short Black Coat)

Those full-size orders, decorations, and medals that are suspended from the medal bar are worn attached to the left side of the coat. Only one full-size neck badge should be worn, suspended from a full-width ribbon. The ribbon is worn under the shirt collar so that the badge rests on the tie immediately below the knot. Up to four stars of orders may be worn on the tailcoat, and only one star on the director's short black coat, attached to the left side below the insignia on the medal bar.

Women (Afternoon Dress)

Those full-size orders, decorations, and medals that are suspended from a medal bar are worn attached to the left side of the dress. If in possession of only one such award, it may be worn on a bow. Only one full-size neck badge should be worn. This should be worn on a bow above the medal bar on the left shoulder. Only one star of an order should be worn on the left side of the dress below all other insignia.

Business Suit

Men

Those full-size orders, decorations, and medals that are suspended from a medal bar are worn attached to the left side of the coat. Only one neck badge should be worn, suspended from a full-width ribbon. The ribbon is worn under the shirt collar so that the badge rests on the tie, immediately below the knot. The stars of orders should not be worn with business suits.

Women

When attending a function where men are wearing business suits, women should, if the function is during the day, wear their full-size orders, decorations, and medals that are worn from a medal bar. If the function is in the evening, the miniatures may be worn. Only one full-size neck badge should be worn. This can be worn on a bow on the left shoulder above the medal bar. The stars of orders should not be worn on these occasions.

Uniforms

Members of uniformed organizations such as the Canadian Forces, police forces, St. John Ambulance, the Corps of Commissionaires, et cetera, should wear the insignia of their orders, decorations, and medals as laid down in the dress regulations of the organization to which they belong.

Overcoats

Only those full-size orders, decorations, and medals mounted on a medal bar should be worn on an overcoat at outdoor functions such as Remembrance Day. Neither neck badges nor stars of orders should be worn (they may be worn underneath). Generally, orders, decorations, and medals should *not* be worn on an overcoat, since they are much more vulnerable to becoming wet and damaged.

Lapel Badges

Included in the insignia of some orders and decorations is a lapel badge or boutonniere. This badge may be worn on the left lapel of the coat with any order of dress at any time when full-size or miniature insignia or the undress ribbon is not being worn. Women may wear this badge in a similar position on the dress or jacket. Only one such badge should be worn at any single time.

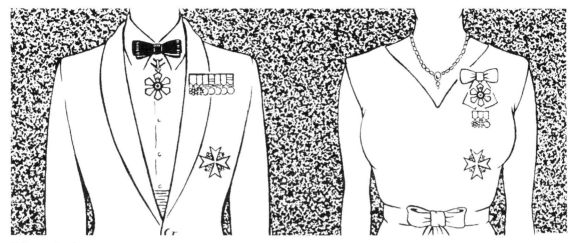

Dinner Jacket

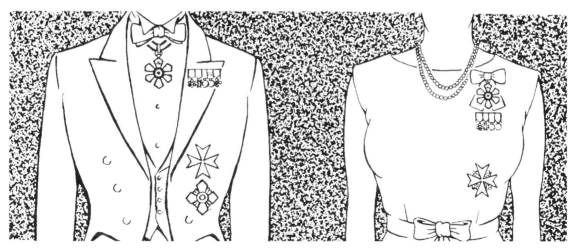

Full Evening Dress

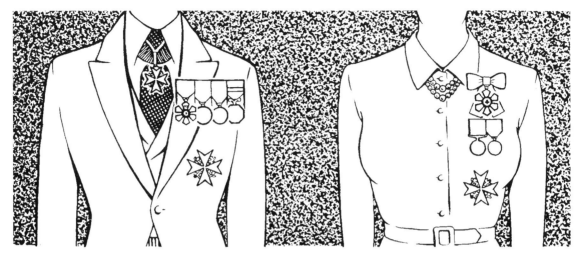

Morning Suit

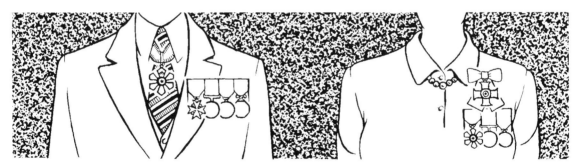

Business Suit

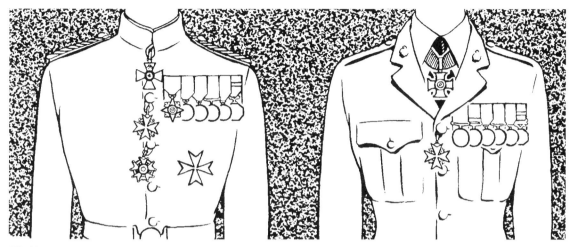

Uniforms

13 Chart of Ribbons, Ribbon Insignia, and Commendation Bars

RIBBONS

Victoria Cross (VC)

Cross of Valour (CV)

Companion of the Order of Canada (CC)

Officer of the Order of Canada (OC)

Member of the Order of Canada (CM)

Commander of the Order of Military Merit (CMM)

Commander of the Order of Merit of the Police Forces (COM)

Commander of the Royal Victorian Order (CVO)

Officer of the Order of Military Merit (OMM)

Officer of the Order of Merit of the Police Forces (OOM)

Lieutenant of the Royal Victorian Order (LVO)

Member of the Order of Military Merit (MMM)

Member of the Order of Merit of the Police Forces (MOM)

Member of the Royal Victorian Order (MVO)

Most Venerable Order of St. John of Jerusalem (All Grades)

L'Ordre national du Québec (All Grades) (GOQ, OQ, CQ)

Saskatchewan Order of Merit (SOM)

Order of Ontario (O.Ont.)

Order of British Columbia (OBC)

Alberta Order of Excellence (AOE)

Order of Prince Edward Island (OPEI)

Manitoba Order of Merit (O.Mb.)

Order of New Brunswick (ONB)

Order of Nova Scotia (ONS)

Order of Newfoundland and Labrador (ONL)

Star of Military Valour (SMV)

Star of Courage (SC)

Meritorious Service Cross (MSC) (Military)

Meritorious Service Cross (MSC) (Civil)

Medal of Military Valour (MMV)

Medal of Bravery (MB)

Meritorious Service Medal (MSM) (Military)

Meritorious Service Medal (MSM) (Civil)

Royal Victorian Medal (RVM)

Gulf and Kuwait Medal

Somalia Medal

South West Asia Service
Medal

General Campaign Star

General Service Medal

Special Service Medal

Canadian Peacekeeping
Service Medal

UN Emergency Force
Medal, UNEF

UN Truce Supervision
Organization in
Palestine and Observer
Group in Lebanon,
UNTSO

UN Good Offices Mission
in Afghanistan and
Pakistan, UNGOMAP

UN Military Observation
Group in India and
Pakistan, UNMOGIP

UN Organization in the
Congo, ONUC

UN Temporary Executive
Authority in West New
Guinea, UNTEA

UN Yemen Observation
Mission, UNYOM

UN Force in Cyprus,
UNFICYP

UN India/Pakistan
Observation Mission,
UNIPOM

UN Emergency Force
Middle East, UNEFME

UN Disengagement
Observation Force Golan
Heights, UNDOF

UN Interim Force in
Lebanon, UNFIL

UN Military Observation
Group in Iran/Iraq,
UNIMOG

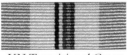

UN Transitional Group
Namibia, UNTAG

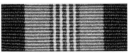

UN Observer Group
in Central America,
ONUCA

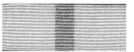

UN Iraq/Kuwait Observer Mission, UNIKOM

UN Angola Verification Mission, UNAVEM

UN Mission for the Referendum in Western Sahara, MINURSO

UN Observer Mission in El Salvador, ONUSAL

UN Protection Force (Yugoslavia), UNPROFOR

UN Advance Mission in Cambodia, UNAMIC

UN Transitional Authority in Cambodia, UNTAC

UN Operation in Somalia, UNSOM

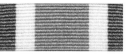

UN Operation in Mozambique, ONUMOZ

UN Observation Mission in Uganda/Rwanda, UNAMUR

UN Assistance Mission in Rwanda, UNAMIR

UN Mission in Haiti, UNMIH

UN Verification of Human Rights in Guatemala, MINUGUA

UN Mission Central African Republic, MINURCA

UN Preventative Deployment Force (Macedonia), UNPREDEP

UN Mission in Bosnia and Herzegovina, UNMIBH

UN Military Observer Mission in Prevlaka (Croatia), UNMOP

UN Interim Administration Mission in Kosovo, UNMIK

UN Observer Mission in Sierra Leone/UN Mission in Sierra Leone, UNOMSIL/UNAMSIL

UN Assistance Mission East Timor/UN Transitional Authority East Timor, UNAMET/UNTAET

The Beginner's Guide to Canadian Honours

UN Mission in the Democratic Republic of Congo, MONUC

UN Mission in Ethiopia and Eritrea, UNMEE

UN Stabilization Mission in Haiti, MINUSTAH

UN Operation in Ivory Coast, ONUCI

UN Mission in Sudan, UNMIS

UN Headquarters Service, UNHQ

NATO Former Yugoslavia

NATO Kosovo

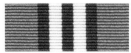

NATO Former Yugoslavia, Republic of Macedonia

NATO Article 5, Operation Eagle Assist

NATO Article 5, Operation Active Endeavour

NATO Non-Article 5, Balkans

NATO Non-Article 5, NTM-IRAQ, Training Implementation Mission and Training Mission in Iraq

NATO Non-Article 5, AMIS, Logistical Support to the African Union Mission in Sudan

International Commission for Supervision and Control Indochina, ICSC

International Commission for Control and Supervision Vietnam, ICCS

Multinational Force Observer Medal (MFO)

European Community Monitor Mission Yugoslavia, ECMMY

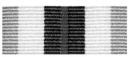

International Force East Timor, INTERFET

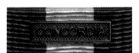

European Security and Defence Policy Service Medal, Concordia

*European Security and
Defence Policy Service
Medal, Artemis*

*Canada Centennial
(1967) Medal*

*Queen Elizabeth II Silver
Jubilee (1977) Medal*

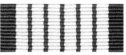

*Canada 125th
Anniversary of
Confederation (1992)
Medal*

*Queen Elizabeth II
Golden Jubilee (2002)
Medal*

*Royal Canadian
Mounted Police Long
Service Medal*

*Canadian Forces
Decoration (CD)*

*Police Exemplary Service
Medal*

*Correctional Service
Exemplary Medal*

*Fire Services Exemplary
Service Medal*

*Coast Guard Exemplary
Service Medal*

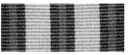

*Emergency Medical
Services Exemplary
Service Medal*

*Peace Officer Exemplary
Service Medal*

*Queen's Medal for
Champion Shot Medal*

*Order of St. John Long
Service Medal*

*Canadian Corps of
Commissionaires Long
Service Medal*

*Saskatchewan Centennial
Medal*

*Alberta Centennial
Medal*

RIBBON INSIGNIA

Mention in Dispatches

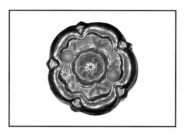

Rosette

Numeral 2

Numeral 3

Silver Maple Leaf

Gold Maple Leaf

Red Maple Leaf

COMMENDATION BARS

Commander in Chief Commendation

Veterans Affairs Canada Commendation

Viceregal Commendation

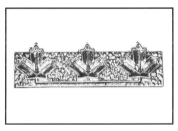

Chief of the Defence Staff Commendation

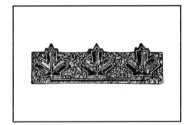

Command Commendation

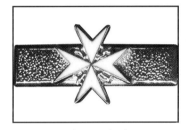

St. John Ambulance Chancellor's Commendation

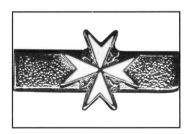

St. John Ambulance Provincial Commendation

Glossary

Advisory Council: The group of officials who decide which Canadians should receive the various Canadian orders, decorations, and medals. Each set of awards has its own Advisory Council or Advisory Committee.

Award: A general term for an order, decoration, or medal. All of these are types of official awards.

Badge: The insignia or medal that is given to those who receive an honour. It is usually made of gold or silver.

Certificate: The piece of paper that is given to those who have been awarded a Canadian honour. It has their name on it and is signed by the Queen or the governor general.

Chancellery of Honours: The office that administers the Canadian honours system.

Chancellor: The person who presents the badge of the Order of Canada to those who have been appointed to the order.

Citation: The short paragraph that describes why a person has been awarded a particular Canadian honour.

Decoration: A type of award given for bravery or meritorious service.

Insignia: The medal or badge that is given to those who receive an honour.

Medal: A type of award usually given for serving in a United Nations peacekeeping mission or in a war. Sometimes medals are presented to commemorate an event such as a coronation. They are also given for long service.

Motto: The saying that describes those who have been appointed to an order. For the Order of Canada the motto is "They desire a better country."

Nomination Form: The piece of paper that a person can fill in to nominate someone to receive a Canadian honour.

Nominator: Any person who writes to nominate someone to receive a Canadian honour.

Obverse: The side of a medal, decoration, or award that bears the head or principal design. Sometimes this is called the front of the medal.

Order: A type of award for outstanding contributions over a long period.

Reverse: The side of a medal, decoration, or award that bears the secondary design. Sometimes this is called the back of the medal.

Ribbon: The piece of coloured cloth that the badge of a Canadian honour is hung from.

Seal: The piece of paper pressed onto the bottom of an award certificate to make the award official.

Secretary General: The person responsible for operating the Chancellery of Honours and making sure that the honours system functions properly.

Sovereign: Queen Elizabeth II, Queen of Canada, is the sovereign of all the Canadian orders.

Useful Addresses and Internet Links

Chancellery of Canadian Honours
Rideau Hall
1 Sussex Drive
Ottawa, Ontario
K1A 0A4
1–800–465–6890
www.gg.ca

Department of National Defence
Directorate of Honours and Recognition
Major-General George R. Pearkes Building
101 Colonel By Drive
Ottawa, Ontario
K1A 0K2
www.forces.gc.ca/dhh

Further Reading

Blatherwick, John F. *Canadian Orders, Decorations and Medals*. Toronto: Unitrade Press, 2003.

Greaves, Kevin. *The Canadian Heraldry Primer*. Toronto: Dundurn Press, 2004.

McCreery, Christopher. *The Canadian Honours System*. Toronto: Dundurn Press, 2005.

____. *The Order of Canada: Its Origins, History and Development*. Toronto: University of Toronto Press, 2005.

Acknowledgements

This project came about following the publication of my first book, *The Canadian Honours System,* in 2005. A number of readers contacted me and encouraged the writing of a book aimed at young people and those who have little knowledge of Canada's various orders, decorations, and medals.

The general concept for *The Beginner's Guide to Canadian Honours* is drawn from the French publication *Raconte moi la Légion d'honneur* (*Tell Me About the Légion d'honneur*). As the title suggests, this work examines, in an accessible way, the history and purpose of France's Légion d'honneur. It is perhaps the first detailed children's book about honours and provided a solid example to follow.

As with my other books, great credit is owed to Bruce Patterson, St. Laurent herald at the Canadian Heraldic Authority, and Captain Carl Gauthier from the Department of National Defence. Both edited the early versions of the text and provided me with great encouragement. Similarly, I am indebted to Marie-Paule Throne from Rideau Hall, who helped me ensure that the content and language of this book were suitable for young people. The late Mary de Bellefeuille-Percy, formerly director of honours at Rideau Hall, helped to ensure the accuracy of the text. Sincere thanks are owed to the Department of National Defence and the Office of the Governor General for providing the vast majority of photographs included in this book.

Throughout this project I have been fortunate to have had the support of many friends. In particular, General John de Chastelain was the first friend to champion the publication of a work aimed at young people. My dear friend, Savita Custead, who is a child educator, has been pushing for this for a number of years with constant questions, the most frequent one being "what's an honour?" Other supporters include Dr. D. Michael Jackson, Joyce Bryant, Father Jacques Monet, the Reverend Dr. Peter Galloway, Sean Morency, Lindsay Maynard, Kevin MacLeod, Claire Boudreau, Darrel Kennedy, Robb Watt, John Geiger, and of course my parents, Paul and Sharon.

Lastly, thanks are owed to my brother, Jonathan. Whether it is working together on re-building a Corvair or engaging in other antics, he is a true best friend and supportive sibling.